Copyright 2019
All rights reserved
ISBN: 978-1-64606-351-2
Published by Happy Lifestyle Online

All rights reserved. No part of this book may be reproduced or transmitted in any form or by any means, electronic or mechanical, including photocopying, recording or by an information storage and retrieval system - except by a reviewer who may quote brief passages in a review to be printed in a magazine or blog - with permission in writing from the author.

Instagram.com/UnicornJazzBrand

UnicornJazz.com

Unicorn Jazz

Lisa Caprelli, Author
Davey Villalobos, Illustrator

Dedication by the Author:

Inspired by my beautiful niece, Jasmine, who always has a positive outlook in life and always sees the best in others.
May you never take a single day for granted!
And for all you unicorn lovers, never stop believing.

Dedication by the Illustrator:

For my girls, Avery and Eleya… all my love.

Once there was a unicorn named Jazz
She was kind, friendly, and a bit shy.

She looked like a horse,
but with a colorful, golden horn
in the middle of her head.

Her father was **Big** and Strong.

Her mother was **kind** and clever.

Deep inside Jazz wanted to be a singer.

She was amazed when her mother sang to her. Her mother's voice made her feel brave.

Although Jazz was talented like her mother, she was afraid to sing. She was too shy.

But whenever Jazz was alone, she sang out loud to herself, the same song her mother sang to her...

"Be HAPPY with your light. You are bold, you shine sooo bright, a Golden ray you're my Sunshine! Let nothing give you fright you are strong your heart is kind. And everyday you're my heart's delight..."

These words made Jazz feel brave.

One day, Jazz and her family moved to a magical land.

↑ Mona the Elephant*

This land had ALL SORTS of animals.

There were birds who sang the sweetest tunes...

along with horses,

giraffes,

lizards and geckos!

Jazz desperately wanted to make friends with these animals but she felt like she didn't belong.

"How am I going to fit in? I don't think anyone likes me here," she sighed.

The unicorn family was not the same as the other animals here.

Unicorns like to sing - a lot!

Whenever Jazz wanted to make new friends, she would sing a silly chant:

"Gonna go out, make a friend or two, laugh with, play with, under skies sooo blue!"

Soon school would start and Jazz was afraid she would not find friends like her.

She tried to make friends with the horses,
but the horses didn't like her.
She did not look like a horse with that big
colorful golden horn on her head.

"You don't look like a real horse," one said.
"Horses do NOT sing," said another.

They did not want to play with her.
The horses just stared at Jazz
and wondered what kind of horse
had a horn on their head.

Jazz walked away and tried to make friends with the giraffes. The giraffes had two tiny horns on their head.

The giraffes told Jazz she was not tall like a giraffe.

They said, "How will you eat the tops of the trees? You can not see as high as we can."

Jazz tried to show them that she could eat the tops of the tree, but the trees were way too tall and her neck was too short.
"They are right, I'm nothing like a giraffe," and she sadly walked away...
Jazz was faster, more colorful, and had just one single horn.
The animals ignored her and Jazz went off in search of new friends.

Soon Jazz found some lizards and geckos.
Some could change colors and blend into objects.
This made them very good at hiding.

"You are probably not very good
at hide and seek," they told her.

Jazz was not able to hide her color.
Although she tried to hide it, it was not
very fun because the gecko always found her.

Jazz told her mother she didn't
want to go to school.
"I am so different. I don't think anyone will like me."

Her mother sang the Unicorn Jazz song
to make Jazz feel better:

"Be happy with your light. You are bold, you shine sooo bright, a Golden ray you're my sunshine! Let nothing give you fright you are strong, your heart is kind and everyday you're my heart's delight..."

Jazz was worried and scared.
With grace, her mother said,"You should love what makes you unique. You are adorable and can sing better than anyone I know, Jazzy girl."

Jazz was so worried about going to school and not making any friends that she wandered into the mountains by herself.

There were no friends to play with in this new place. Jazz felt sad and alone.

Jazz wanted to feel happy, so she sang the song her mother taught her.

As she was singing, a bird flew down.

He was not like other birds.
His feathers were black and white
and not at all colorful.

"Look at you! You have a beautiful voice,"
he said in a raspy voice.

Jazz was surprised.
"Thank you. Who are you?"
she replied bashfully.

Only her Momma had ever said nice
things about her voice.

"My name is Woof!"

"I am a Crow. I know, you must be thinking, "Who would take a name like Woof seriously?"

"I have a name that a dog should have."

Woof continued to stare at Jazz and said, "You, my dear, are an AMAZING singer! Your voice is so, so magical. What I wouldn't give for a voice like yours!"

Stunned, she replied,
"I don't think I'm magical, really...
the other animals don't understand me,
because I look different."

"Hmm, well, you do have a lot of
beauty and color, you know?"
said Woof.

You have a strong, glorious horn!
You sing more beautifully
than any other bird I've ever heard."

Jazz smiled ear to ear.

"The other birds
do not think I am like them," said Woof,

"But that does
not stop me from being who
I want to be. I have a great
memory, too.

Listen to me hum your song."

Instantly, Woof, hummed the
exact tune that Jazz just sang
moments before.

"Be happy with your light.
You are bold,
You shine soooo bright,
A Golden ray
You're my sunshine
Let nothing give you fright
You are strong
Your heart is kind.
And everyday
You're my heart's delight..."

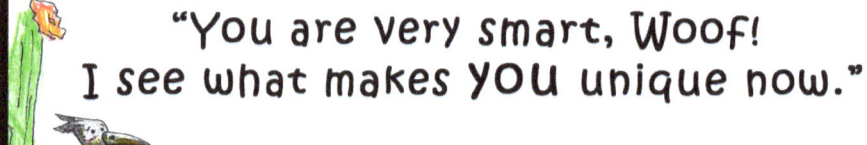

"You are very smart, Woof! I see what makes YOU unique now."

Jazz was happy. She found a friend.

"You should always be proud of what makes you special," said Woof. "I bet, if you showed others your beautiful voice, they would agree."

"I'm not afraid to sing loud," and in a raspy voice, Woof sang:

"What do you do with a friend like yooo-"

They both laughed.
"Maybe you should let me sing. That did not sound very good, but you still had fun doing it, right?"

"Yes, of course. Now you sing," said Woof.
Boldly and loudly, Jazz sang.

The lizards spoke, "You have such
beautiful colors, and sing with
such grace. You can't play hide and seek,
but you can sing?"

The horses spoke. "You aren't a horse. No horse
could sing so beautifully. We are sorry,
we didn't realize how AWESOME you are!
Can you teach us how to sing like you?"

Blushing, Jazz nodded.
"Only if you let me race with you!"

Yay I Say!

They all laughed and were happy.

Jazz did not feel alone anymore.
She was not afraid to show off her talent.

All the animals asked to play games with Jazz:
Play hopscotch with me!
Color with me!
Sing with me!
Dance with me!

Early Concept Drawings

Mona The Elephant

Mona, an Asian Elephant, was among the most popular animals to visit at the zoo. She came to El Paso in 1956 at 700 pounds.

The Asian elephant, is the only living species of the "genus Elephas" and is distributed in the Indian subcontinent and Southeast Asia, from India and Nepal in the west to Borneo in the south.

The El Paso Zoo has a lot of history on its beginnings to where it is now. It is now a regional attraction featuring dynamic conservation education programs and experiences with animals from around the world.

From the Author:

"Let's go see Mona!" That was a common request I had as a little girl and I got to grow up with her, as did many of her fans.

Acknowledgements

This book and Unicorn Jazz's vision would not be possible without many awesome people who contributed!

Family: Jasmine Powers; my momma Hope Hernandez; Tia Lucy Dominguez; Alyssa Ruiz, Lori Caprelli, Chris Herzig, Marcello Funk,

Siblings: Debbie Powers, Suzanne Funk, Ruth Leigh, Mike Hernandez; Sons: Matthew Vasquez-Caprelli, Trey Solomon

Friends: Blake Pinto, Thanecha Anderson, Rachel Unnever, Julie Kasem, Tom Martin, Anna Daugherty, Lorraine Martinez, Donna Hernandez; Luisa, Holda and Joseph Dorsey, Alexis Maron

Last but not Least: My *Woof the Crow's*—these people believed in me:

Cindy Kirkland, Rg Lutz, Chris Herzig, Miguel Barillas, Kerri Kasem, Claudia Dangerfield, Ken Walls, Alex Agahi, Ibonne Demogines, Greg Moore

I BELIEVE IN YOU!
~Woof the Crow

New readers, teachers, counselors, principals and so many more people — we cannot thank you enough for your kindness, love, inspiration, and giving back!

Author & Illustrator Bios

Lisa Caprelli is a Latina mother who enjoys creative writing, teaching and researching to create a culture of communication, fulfillment and happiness. Unicorn Jazz reflects her inquisitive nature of understanding of human behavior. Lisa has a Bachelor's in Social Psychology and is also the host of Happy Lifestyle Online Show.

Born and raised in El Paso, Texas she settled in Orange County, California in 2001. As a writer, marketer and business development leader with

over 25 years of experience, she is called upon for strategy, motivation and inspiration. She has changed her life to become an accomplished author and help others author their own stories.

Lisa enjoys speaking and teaching diverse audiences of all ages, from elementary schools, teens and millennials, to seasoned business professionals.

Lisa is proud mother of two sons, Matthew (a nurse) and Trey (a popular YouTuber—with over 40 million views under the name "TreyJam" on YouTube).

Davey Villalobos resides in El Paso, Texas. He is a proud uncle, baker by trade, avid reader and cycling enthusiast. He has been drawing since he was able to hold a crayon.

Book Summary

Jazz is a dazzling young unicorn with incandescent purple hair, a golden horn and shining hoofs to match. Although quite timid in nature, her most stunning quality is her voice in song. Her melody surpasses and soothes all the other animals who hear her sing. When she and her parents move to a new place for the first time, she finds herself at odds with the other animal members, such as horses and geckos, at school.

While Jazz thought that she and the horses would get along nicely, they didn't seem to accept her due to her peculiar golden horn. Finding no luck making friends with the horses, Jazz approached the giraffes, as they too had horns. But despite this similarity, she was not welcomed among the giraffes because her neck was too short.

After her encounter with the giraffes, Jazz moves on in search of more animal friends, but she can't seem to find her place. Feeling lonely and discouraged, Jazz takes a walk through a forest and begins to sing her heart away when a crow descends to talk to her. Unlike the other animals, the crow believes that Jazz has an incredible voice, splendid hair and an amazing horn.

This interaction gives Jazz the confidence to strut back to school singing and making each and every one of her qualities known. Our majestic friend, who had once seemed to be unfit, teaches a valuable lesson about the power and voice of bringing people together in harmony.

This soothing, colorful book provides a very familiar yet individually unique feeling that any child can relate to. *Unicorn Jazz* reminds us that we are never completely alone.

About the Author

Lisa Caprelli enjoys writing, teaching and researching to create a culture of communication, fulfillment and happiness. *Unicorn Jazz* reflects her inquisitive nature of understanding of human behavior. Lisa has a Bachelor's in Social Psychology and is also the host of Happy Lifestyle Online Show.

Born and raised in El Paso, Texas she settled in Orange County, California in 2001. As a writer, marketer and business development leader with over 25 yrs of experience, she is called upon for strategy, motivation and inspiration to take massive action steps for the work she represents.

Lisa enjoys speaking and teaching diverse audiences of all ages, from elementary schools, teens and millennials, to seasoned business professionals.

"Interviewing people and learning about their successes, experiences and struggles has always been fascinating to me because we have the capacity as human beings to be and do more than we ever thought possible by drawing from other people's perspectives."

Literacy Info

Recommended Reading Level: Grades 3-5
Flesch-Kincaid Grade Level: 2.9
Lexile Range: 500L - 600L
Genres: Fiction, Fantasy
Themes: Diversity, Friendship, Self-Esteem

Unicorn Jazz is a fun, whimsical read-aloud for all ages. For independent readers, this book is most appropriate for children between the ages of 8-10.

Learning Standards

The activities in this Curriculum Guide meet the Common Core State Standards (CCSS) in the areas of Speaking and Listening, Reading Literature and Math. The curriculum is also aligned to the Next Generation Science Standards. Specific standards are noted with each activity.

Discussion Guide

Unicorn Jazz presents valuable messages about self-acceptance, kindness and empathy. The story offers the perfect opportunity to teach students how to make text-to-self connections and identify their own emotions.

Encourage students to think about situations when they may have felt similar to Jazz in the story. Ask questions such as, "How would you describe this feeling? What did you, or someone else, do to make yourself feel better?" Also explore questions related to diversity and inclusion such as, "Why is it important to make others feel welcomed? If someone feels lonely, how can we help them feel included?

Have the students complete the Unicorn Jazz: I Like Me! worksheet as an extension activity for social-emotion competence.

Extension Activities

Language Arts

Have the students define key vocabulary words from the story and identify literal/figurative language from the text. (RL.3.4, RL.4.4, RL.5.4)

**unique
bashfully
delight
gecko
wandered
boldly
glorious**

Jazz sang the beautiful tune, "Be happy with your light. You are bold, you shine so bright. A golden ray, you're my sunshine." Ask the students to think about the figurative language used in the song lyrics. Is Jazz singing about an actual sun? If not, what is being compared to the sun?

Ask students to think about the central message of the story. Have them highlight key phrases from the story that help reveal the story's central message. For example, the character Woof says, "You should always be proud of what makes you special." (p. 18). How does this sentence express what the author wants you to learn from this story?

Science

In the story, each animal has special characteristics. Explore how animals differ in appearance, personality, habitats, etc. in nature. How is each animal unique? (3-LS3-1,LS3.B: Variation of Traits) Use the Unicorn Jazz: Character Map to help students make connections from the text.

Make unicorn slime and observe how chemical reactions turn liquids into solids. (2-PS1-1, PS1.A: Structure and Properties of Matter)

Materials needed:

- Glitter glue (assorted colors)
- Liquid starch
- Mixing bowl
- plastic spoon

Mix 6 ounces (or 1 glue bottle) of glitter glue with 1/4 cup of liquid starch. Stir together until the mixture solidifies. Explore bright, magical color combinations like the beautiful unicorn Jazz!

Writing

Help students express ideas about the story in writing (W.3.4, W.4.4, W.5.4). Use writing prompts such as:

- Think about a time when you had to experience something new. This could be a new school, town, pet, sibling, etc. How did you feel about this experience at first? Did these feelings change as you adjusted to the new experience? Why or why not?

- The character Woof had an unusual name. He was a crow with a name that sounded like a dog's. Is there anything unusual about your name? Where did your name, or nickname come from?

Art, Music and Drama

Let the students color or paint the printable Unicorn Jazz coloring page. Ask them about their color choices. Help them explore ideas about what may be happening in the coloring page scene.

Explore the Unicorn Jazz song and lyrics. How does this song make you feel? Encourage students to write and perform their own song about individuality and self-love.

Turn *Unicorn Jazz* into a class play! Assign characters, or let the children choose. Help the students make masks, costumes, props, etc.

Math

In the story, Jazz did not fit in with the giraffes because her neck was not long enough. Did you know that a giraffe's neck is about 6 feet long? They also have very long legs and short horns on their head. Have the students measure their necks and other body parts such as arms. Compare and graph the results. (2.MD.A.1-4)

I Like Me!

Jazz learned to like herself because she was unique. She liked her beautiful voice, her dazzling horn and her shimmering colors. What makes you unique? Write at least 3 special things about yourself.

I am unique because
_____
_____
_____
_____
_____
_____
_____
_____
_____
_____

Unicorn Jazz Character Map

There were many amazing animals in the story *Unicorn Jazz*. Each animal had their own special characteristics. Think about your favorite character from the story and describe them in the map below.

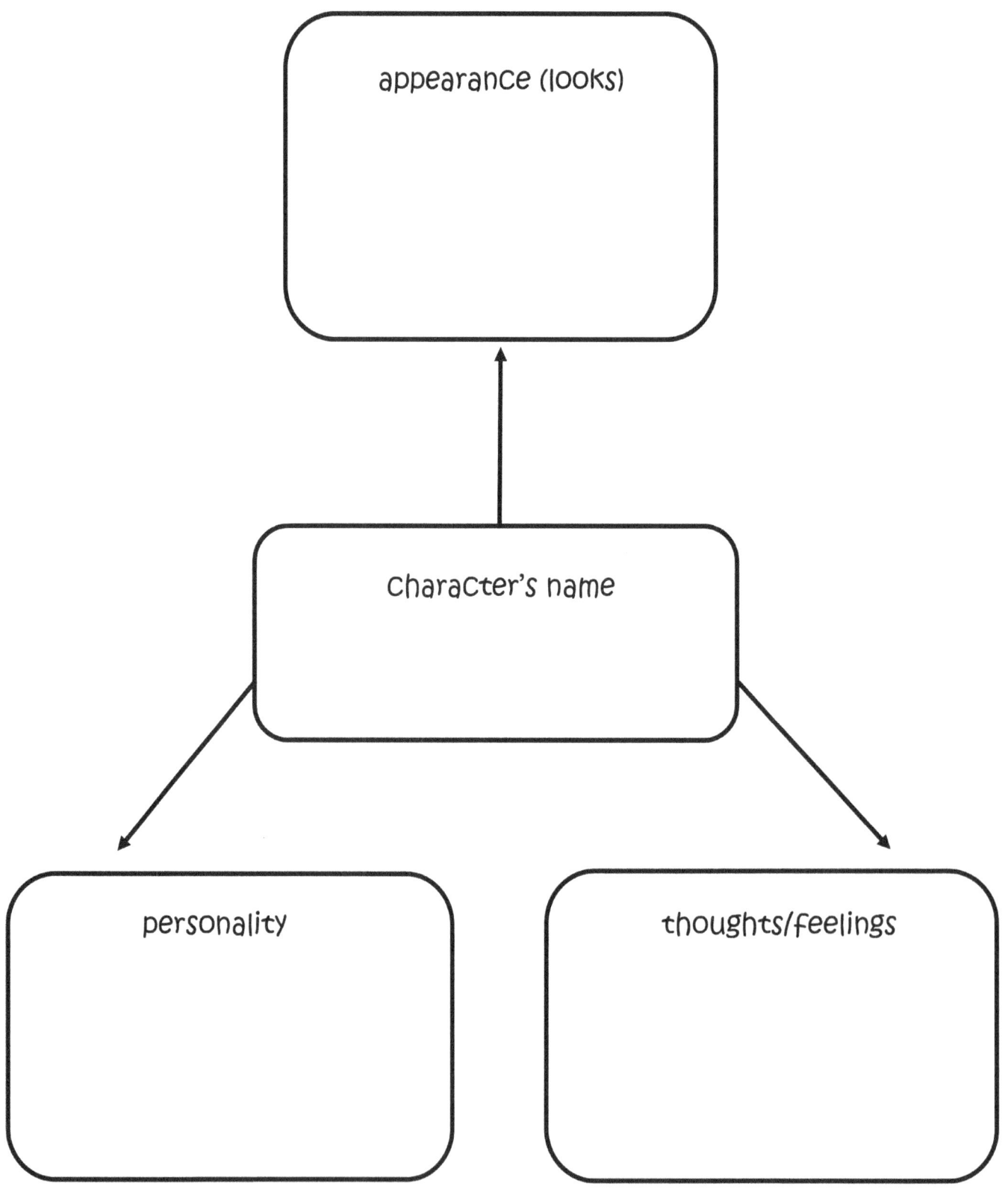

Based on the book **Unicorn Jazz** on Amazon!
Author: Lisa Caprelli
Illustrator: Davey Villalobos

~The End~

(Until the next Unicorn Jazz Book)

Available for sale on Amazon are Unicorn Jazz t-shirts. More products to come like Unicorn Jazz coloring books, Unicorn Jazz gifts, and much more!

Visit often at: UnicornJazz.com and share your messages with us on: Instagram.com/UnicornJazz

Teacher Curriculum Available to accompany this book!

www.ingramcontent.com/pod-product-compliance
Lightning Source LLC
Chambersburg PA
CBHW061129070526
44584CB00033B/4275